CW00767659

ink's
wish

sarah law

Gatehouse Press

www.gatehousepress.com

Published by
Gatehouse Press Limited
90 Earlham Road
Norwich NR2 3HA

www.gatehousepress.com

First Published in 2014 by
Gatehouse Press Limited

ISBN 978-0-9566385-9-5

Cover design by Norwich Designer

Printed and bound in the UK

Contents

Margery's Harbour: A Dramatic Monologue and Songs For Performance with Music by Ken Crandell

Acknowledgements

Thanks to *Stride Magazine* where some Margery poems were published in 2011.

'Margery's Harbour' was first published in my collection *The Lady Chapel* (Exeter: Stride Publications, 2003).

The song lyrics 'How Can I Begin', 'That a Woman Might Speak One Hour [song lyric version]', 'Song of the Senses [song lyric version]', 'Margery's Tears' and 'Margery's Travels' were written by me and set to music by Ken Crandell for a performance at Wymondham Abbey in May 2012.

The text for multi-voice performance, 'When I speak these words', was written and performed at a collaborative creative practice day for The Facility (Centre for Creative Practice as Research), London Metropolitan University, January 2011.

Poems from the collection were read and discussed at Great Writing Conference, Imperial College London, June 2012.

The poem 'Woman of Rome' is selected for publication in the anthology *The Poet's Search for God* (Eyewear Press, 2014).

Thanks to London Metropolitan University for a short period of Teaching Relief granted in order to pursue my interest in Kempe.

And thank you Kev for your support throughout.

Introduction: Meeting Margery

More than any other medieval woman visionary, Margery Kempe of Lynn (*c.* 1373–1438) is a figure who inspires divided responses. Is she in fact a mystic or a menace,[1] her spiritual experience false or genuine (or from God or the devil)? The dichotomizing tendency begins during her lifetime and is documented in her *Book*: 'Eyther thu art a ryth good woman er ellys a ryth wikked woman'.[2] There is also an image of Margery Kempe in popular culture which is hard to escape, that of 'a lady ... well known for her – shall we say – "spiritual problems"'; a type of needy, probably single woman who rather cruelly becomes the butt of clerical jokes.

According to Canon Maclean's 1996 lecture, 'everyone knows Margery was difficult to take. People who know little more than her name or at the most have merely dipped into her book, are always quite clear she was an oddity. They know she went around weeping and howling and persecuting everyone who failed to see her coming, especially the poor wretched clergy. A menace almost certainly.'

That a number of people 'failed to see her coming', both during her lifetime, and in the middle of the twentieth century when her manuscript was discovered in full, indicates a certain quality of shock about Margery Kempe. Should Kempe's life and writing be considered scandalous or somehow exemplary? As Dana Bagshaw in her play about Kempe has her say: 'Am I blessed? / Or am I cursed?'[3]

A fifteenth-century visionary from King's Lynn (then Bishop's Lynn) who is considered to have 'written' (via

---

1. Fr. Michael Maclean, lecture, 'Margery Kempe: Mystic or Menace' (Community of All Hallows Press, 1996).
2. *The Book of Margery Kempe*, Norton Critical Editions (London: W.W. Norton & co., 2001), Chapter 47, p. 113.
3. Dana Bagshawe, *Cell Talk* (London: Radius, 2002), p. 9.

dictation) the first autobiography in English, Margery Kempe, like her older contemporary Julian of Norwich, is today studied as a literary figure, a proto-feminist; her book a challenging text, a spiritual record, an early narrative of the self. Her life and work is the subject of academic research but also of artistic interpretation. Like Julian, her 'book' had lain unconsidered for several centuries until it was subject to a renaissance of interest in the twentieth century. However there are some notable differences between the two texts and their respective authors, and also in the ways in which each has been received and, increasingly, interpreted. Julian of Norwich as an anchoress was a 'still centre', living a life of stability, who others sought for advice; her visions propelled her inwards, and she considered their implications (some with bold development of the concept of Jesus as mother) for many years before completing her text. Margery, by contrast, became distinctly mobile after her husband agreed to a vow of celibacy: she not only went on major pilgrimages (to Europe and the Holy Land) but also frequently sought out advisors closer to home for support and spiritual discernment. As is documented in Margery's book,[4] Julian was one of those to whom she went for such spiritual advice and she seems to have received steadfast (and characteristic in terms of Julian's own writing) recommendations of patience and trust. The meeting is the subject of a number of contemporary works, including Dana Bagshaw's *Cell Talk* and my own poem 'Margery's Harbour'.

The 'shock' of Margery, the ability to disturb, subvert or indeed provoke laughter began – in contemporary reception, at least – with the discovery of the complete text of her autobiography in 1934. Prior to the recovery of this manuscript, Margery Kempe had only been known through selected extracts from her book. It was thought that she had been another anchoress, writing of her spiritual insights from an authorised position (of stability and solitude)

4. See *The Book of Margery Kempe*, Chapter 40.

within the church. But embarrassment and reversal were the consequences of knowing that Kempe was far less stable than carefully selected extracts would suggest.

Now we know that Kempe was a visionary on the move, devoting much of her life, post-vow of chastity with her husband, as a pilgrim. A pilgrimage is not an unusual activity per se in fifteenth-century Europe (and beyond) but Margery's pilgrimages were many, long, causing notable manifestations of her already marked affective piety, and creating social ruptures within her pilgrimage community. Marion Glasscoe usefully identifies the pilgrimage state as a 'liminoid' one: 'a means, which, as it cuts across the structures and divisions of society, may enable the self to be restructured both in interior awareness of the faith and external relations with fellow pilgrims'.[5]

This quality of the liminal and the misfit which we can find in Margery Kempe is largely what attracted me to her as a subject for poetry. It is a quality identified by medievalist and cultural theorist Caroline Dinshaw as 'queer'; especially in Kempe's skewing of conventional social, dress (she felt compelled to wear white, after years as a fashionable wife), and conversational strategies, and in her 'queering', through unexpectedness and instability, relationships between self and other throughout her text. For Dinshaw, queerness is a misfit's state: 'Queerness is just that relation of unfittingness, disjunctiveness – that uncategorizability, that being-left-out … The rubric queer names disjunctives, both within her individual person and between her person and established social forms.'[6]

Margery Kempe has already been the subject of creative interpretations as well as critical ones. Notable examples include Robert Gluck's multi-strand and innovative novel, *Margery Kempe* (Serpent's Tail, 1995), various plays including

5. Marion Glasscoe, *English Medieval Mystics, Games of Faith* (London: Longman, 1993), p. 281.
6. Caroline Dinshaw, *Getting Medieval, Sexualities and Communities, Pre- and Postmodern* (North Carolina: Duke University Press, 1999), p. 158.

Dana Bagshawe's *Cell Talk* (Radius, 1992), and also poetry: twentieth-century poet Howard Nemerov's poem 'Margery Kempe' (in his 1947 collection *Guide to the Ruins*) includes her own memorable exclamation, 'Alas, that ever I sinned! It is right merry in Heaven'. My own poetry seeks to explore and meet with Margery on various levels, including the reflective, the spiritual, the dramatic and comical, and engages with her autobiography, if tangentially. I make no claims for historical accuracy in either event or turn of phrase, although I have on occasion used short quotations from Kempe's *Book*. I write largely though loosely from Kempe's perspective, aware that such a point of view could be construed as appropriation. I am fascinated by Kempe's waywardness, her conviction, her passion, her tears, her ongoing identity as a difficult misfit, and her longing to have her experiences written down and given to others for their own meditation. It has been a pleasure to journey with her, and to sing, read and write of her notable life.

Sarah Law
February 2013

Salt on Silk

Tonight the drizzle
Of hot salt on silk;
A spilt dish of contrition.

Her tears are not corrosive
but distressing to flat art:
Now, her dress's dye –

Blotted, its prettiness swollen
to great dark swirls. She
spots a galaxy onto her lap,

wonders at the miracle of words.

Margery's Soundings

Wrench of a blood bath melon,
the baby, the baby, the baby
croons in her cradle, the pain
it will fade, all the look of
solid gold but empty tin –

that's my heart, a resounding
hollow, an ache that stains,
a rag-tag rattle. O I am damned,
the furnace of the future is
annihilating me. Pray God

to make an end, to cut the
lively cord. To sound out nothing.

He comes when I am least expecting,
body and soul crescent moons,
swatched wands. He sits,
a purple blood-of-lent garment
swathing the body. My daughter,
My Daughter, why then
have you forsaken me, when I
have never left you. Thus his words
not argument, but balm on brow –
a fuller sphere than any of my tears,

no caustic salt – just blood,
milk, sustenance of water.

The Lightning Plan

sche saw veryly how the eyr openyd as brygth as ony levyn,[1] and he stey up into the eyr...

He rose
to a cracked-heart sky

Light shafting
from its blue wound

Never forsake ye
the gravity of love

Words having furled
from his mouth, and lightening

Crashing its pattern
onto her past.

He is a rose
and she is his path

Nobody knows
how such light lasts

1.   **levyn,** lightning

Alas That Ever

I fell into despair
like a maiden into unsuitable love:
compelling, elemental, or so it felt.

The rain teamed inside my susceptible skin.
The subsequent tale was unspeakable,
I'd committed

    a gap in the narrative.
The page fused together with petals,
the answer erased. The very question

queered against its discourse; hidden
in the text, an optical delusion, as desires
so often are. I couldn't confess it,

but those who wrote my story
fleshed me out: a fiery kiss, a stillborn child;
me party to a theft; me greedy, frantic, going wild –

Here is a silence silver as a swan.
On her blank feathers a vibrancy;
the film reel of your stories flutters there,
slips and dissolves into the lake.

A Priest Got Lost in a Forest

A priest got lost in a forest towards the middle of the afternoon. Winter was nigh, and the light was at a special slant of ambiguity. He turned about and about but couldn't find the path, trodden as it was with pins and needles though no compass. He knew he'd already said Mass, so the problem wasn't one of rush, but purely of direction (was he going out or coming home?). Overhead, memories rustled. Sidelines flapped. A shred of ego flisked ahead. The echo of a sigh. An invitation…was it his own? He loved the sound of a man's voice, and walked that way. The outline of an Adam's apple shaped the sky. He smiled. But squirrels shot pellets at his back. He gathered his rough woollen cloak about his body, and pressed on. He had to admit, he was getting peckish himself. If only there was a fruit tree, among the rough green sentinels; if only it bore apples or sweet pears. And soon enough he came upon a clearing, where a rustle of leaves revealed the fruits he craved.

As he ate, the juice slid like a track of light across his face. It daubed his robes, unsublimated grace, a grateful trickle. He sang to himself: he was lost but had found hidden treasure. The forest had mazed him but sustained him; he was resting in the crook of its arm, in the palms of its unfolded prayers. He tarried and grew by a fruity osmosis. The clouds shed water, gentle. He'd never worked with animals, children or women. Well children he knew as he slid baptismal water's light upon them. They hardly ever paid him. Animals were outside the church; and here was a gloss-brown bear, as instinctual as faith. He shared his fare with him.

It's true there was a flicker of white cloth. A light entextured. A word in a weave. Was it a woman? A princess, slipped from the kitchen door, following the unofficial vortex of her life, donning wedding garb in celebration. Laying on moss and soft fallen trunk, the priest smiled once more. A woman as a white cloth as a widow as a song. Such surrender to the unconventional rain.

Life on a Limb

As though a phantom limb
and not my own
the names of God
inscribed upon its cast

my broken leg is numbly
stepping out
across the ocean floor
the donkey's back

a lesson out of class
and local term
the pilgrim pack's diurnal
and my heart beats fast.

Happiness Writes White

It is, in her way, an erasure of self: those white folds replacing the patterns of life hitherto. Chromatic ensembles to snow pure simplicity. The overdone 'drag' of the newly enstated, the bridal, the vowed-to-enclosure, the clean-again mum. Margery doesn't succumb to the slashes of category. She's a slave to the son. In white, she's renewed. In her *big white dress*, she's begun to undo herself. Us alongside: these panels, these fittings and stitches – the panoply played by society: spots! Stripes! And circles … all gone, and emerged for the dubious different pleasures they stood for.

Margery sits, and sometimes rolls on the ground in a fit of contrition. By being OTT she becomes benign, the smile-raiser, the giver of tears who washes all the black and red tapes away from the crime scene. By dressing OTT she shows the little schemes we all fall prey to up as dull, constricting – and still never doing their job as the guardians of sense.

Better to be accused of false bridery than damned for frivolous conformity to the mad world's ways.

Beads of Light

Beads of Light
buoy her over
another rough ocean
and the blue moon
of her mission

Beads of light
on the porcelain face
of Mary, grieving
for the broken hearted,
memorial stars aligned.

Margery gives, receives
pearly strings of prayers;
glimpses of the bright
spots in the soul's scan:

Fracture, pin-hole wisdom,
beads of light as runway lights –
flying the night planes home.

The Holy Pretender

That's her, she's great
with child or the eyes of a child;
she's better with children
than regular souls, whom she troubles
by drag of a dress and unholy
address, which yet unsettles –

She is a woman pretending
to be a woman all blessed and chosen,
a wisp of contractual widowhood;
howling – like wind in a tunnel, she loves
to be cunning, and awful though bullying is
she assumes it as sword
to a sullied episcopate, or
the true word of Pretender:

She is a Margery-Woman pretending to vision
when she is the spectacle, offering vehicle,
she is pretending to Holiness,
reaching the shore with attention and prayer.

Meshes of Margery

Sometimes she couldn't tell
whether she woke or dreamt. That circle
like the cliff-side path, followed
her lost scent. The dropped flower,
the key hidden under the tongue,
the mirror for a face. These came along.
Once she woke and He was there,
at her bedside. He was more than wine,
He was a vine, a key, a ministry,
He said she was divine. Sometimes,
she couldn't tell the question she should pose,
her mouth stoppered with petals, fruits,
the balcony full of sweet breezes
making her swoon. She learned to cleave
to his strong heart. His smile was more
than wine in a grand chalice, or an answer,
so she followed him. He taught her to adore.
Dreams within the veil of dreams. She
who is the lost chord of a hymn, must sing
that love is proven by a fall. That there is
a world of reflection. Severance is only
the early story. Flutter your eyes,
unlock the living room windows, door,
                              walk on.

Woman of Rome

Here I am, not belonging
to anyone at all, except,
perhaps, a Divinity who listens
like a baby in the womb,
a lover to beloved –
I'm calling in the song's words:
Who am I to tell of mystery.
She raises the stone cup and says
drink me. All the birds fly up,
merriness in heaven-on-the-wing.

Drink me. All the birds fly up,
she raises the stone cup. And says
Who am I to tell of mystery.
I'm calling in the song's words:
lover, to beloved,
like a baby in the womb,
perhaps. A Divinity who listens
to anyone at all. Except
here I am. Not belonging.
Still the birds fly home.

Compostella Shots

The end of the world – at least
of Europe in its medieval melting-pot.
Margery in Compostella, spending her time,
earning her shell. In time she will unfurl.

The rain falls and the narrow cobbles gleam,
wine is offered, sustenance and sacrifice.
Margery slips outside and her tears mingle
with the slanting grief of heaven.

Here she can almost smell the sea:
the salt soup of the world which slow-boiled life
into swimming, then creeping sentience,
stars on a dark cloth: heart brimful.

Back to the great God's house. Its holiness
Swirls under rich stone ribs. All
the petty pilgrims gather up their prayers,
exhale. The golden censor swings

across the long body of the nave,
dispersing incense. Together
the scented, silent intercessions mingle
and become acceptable. Margery

slips from her own flesh into a veil
between shell and the beating
muscle of the heart. The golden
sand she lands on feels like home.

To Trouble You

It was the cause He issued: come to trouble you
enough that you broke rank. Nothing but trouble. You

challenged the clergy, crossed the borders, ordered
this creature be allowed to weep and trouble you.

You are a wicked woman. No, it's you
who are a wicked man. The genders trouble you,

each second person slipping into hinterland –
the hymn you warble, hurt you roared. In trouble. You.

Taken to court, the accusations claw at you,
but Margery does more than merely muddle through.

Her words rise up like swans, white, heart-shaped, strong,
this Margery makes language. You're in trouble, too.

Up Her Sleeves

Piquant, the folds fall
    fleshed human follies –
    she's seen them all.

Love's a hot narcotic,
    a rest from the diurnal,
    the gossip's only topic.

Red as the eternal
    pulse along the cotton's vein,
    blushing's gone internal,

my sartorial loss, but heaven's gain,
    these naked wrists, these calloused feet,
    they call me witch, insane,

yet in the stripped down streets,
    this earth under her star-wide skirt of sky,
    we meet.

A Taken Cake

A cake on a walk, with a bottle
of brewery beer. My husband, he
who had been hot and hard
to manage, even for I who hold

the ropes in love and commerce –
he and I brought forth our brood,
all vibrant art: this worked to make me
mad. As mad as the rags in a breeze

or the ragged cry of the cat.
Thus love induced herself to me.
And he grew withered on the vine
of our togetherness. And it was time

for a new contract. John, dear John,
we took new vows before the bishop.
a husband vowed to leave me be,
he took persuasion. In the field,

holding his beer and cake, this man
asks whether I value his life over
my chastity, new budded. The truth
I told him. And he –

He gave me over unto Love.

Roaring Girl

The roar of a girl –
Lioness grieving
Goddess pleading
Pain enfolding
Hot-hand-holding

Rod for heaven's back –

Small dews,
Drawn to a vortex

Whale's plume
Lovers' cortex

Hymn books
Torn to chapel floor

Roaring –

She,
    The awful resonance of flesh
The thorn engorged
The spirit, sobbing –
Spirit-blessed:

A wild girl calling for her God.

That a Woman Might Speak One Hour on the Love of God

He, lyftyng vp hys handys & blyssyng hym, seyd, 'Benedicite. What cowd a woman ocupyn an owyr er tweyn owyrs in the lofe of owyr Lord?'

Five minutes with your palms up-cupped
I river them with women's words

A minute at the burnished table
here starts *Margery's main fable*:

Twenty minutes at my narrative
of priests and bishops. Who arrive
in unknown places and get lost
for ten long minutes. Half-lit forests.

Four minutes' midnight warning.
A *Pater Noster*'s worth of mourning.

Six sixty seconds of delighting
with more laughter than affrighting –

Then a moment's hesitation –
(three *Hail Marys* and a *Station*)
and my monologue to finish,
decade's worth of beaded minutes.

Thus as woman will I speak.

Now press repeat.

A Fluttering Dove

You bend your knees, he lifts
as though together you're a
strong man raising metal bars –

you chant the words, he sifts
humanity's sounds through
liturgy's net. A silver shoal

of prayer-fish fillip
onto the altar. Hush.
They are to moving tears

as birds to the raised-up hope.
You bow your head. He lifts
this consecrated world of ours

before your gaze, which drifts,
as motes within the sunlight.
Sun streams onto white disc:

which flutters, a dove awakened,
at its moment of becoming
conscious, warm and beckoning you,
your marvellous heart.

By this Sweet Smell, Thou Mayest Well Know

Honey and hops –
the soul's sweet brew.

A petal partly crushed,
that dream you can't remember.

Synaesthesia. Song.
I knew him all along.

Ink, sweat and tears,
the twisted rope of years

wrung into words,
my scribes – bright birds

candlewax and water
sanctity's elements.

Salt and bitter and wood,
a woman on a boat,

telling tales, taking breath,
she's the sea's sweet liquor

talking to me. Heart, crossed
with prayer and heat.

How to Weep

Drink an ocean.
     Let it raise your gorge
like a whale's spume.
     Swallow it down.

Tilt your full head back.
     Gaze at the clouds.
Let your eyes pool, reflect
     the air's wide ache.

Memory will stream her pictures
     each a sob; holy shadows
stoop like dark-cloud figures
     over the rivering past:

Stand up, stretch wide, cry out.
     Lie prone and cruciform, cry down
the sorry heavens.
     This is your refrain.

Gather grief into a pilgrim's bundle;
     the cloud will burst again.
Drink an ocean. Vanish and
     disperse yourself. Ascend.

Creation Wick

When God made Margery
He put a wick inside her,

rough and long as a well-lived life
tough to light and hard to snuff,

causing a glow. Don't put your hands
onto her mouth, she'll flame you.

Clear a space, lest she kiss fire,
a rose gold love chain; rope you

to the sanctuary. She's her own wax,
a lyrical roar, a calling. Look, Mad

Donna, at her pearly tears,
spilling from her column of witness,

pooling, luminescent, and still here.

The Shock of the Few

He does not call to many
but to all. He does not want

starvation, but a fullness in the breast,
oiled hair, hands at rest.

Yet this ship has those who stay up late,
watching the waves' night-blackness, the trace

of starlight scribbled on their curves
the clouds' luminous grey. Those few who pray

forgetful of self, of many lives undone.
Brows furrow beads of perseverance.

In the sky, such droplets form and dazzle,
hidden sockets for electric grace.

Life on a Limb II

Salt, tar, filthy rags, songs –
a sense of momentum

seasick Mrs. Kempe aloft
spews prayers, like a flag
pulsed in the cross-channel breeze

*

Margery pours the chorus –
a cluster of pilgrims
sweat the verses

*

Cold stone, sluts of dust
splats of wax

set me as a seal
upon your unwise heart

*

Fetal pummelling

*

The mind stained
a distressed art –

touch of the moderns

*

red-faced
red wine
cup of clay -
she would
be the first

*

Bless me father
for I have

*

These ears are so thirsty
for the again-and-again
of *you are holy*

*

The hand writes dry
but life unspools its words
and you will scribble.

A Haircloth in Thine Heart

The scribble of its itch against the ribs;
penitent striations, muscle
of continuous confession.

I am, I am, I am
a waltz across the body:
a sin, a sin, a sin

Veil her face, let it glimmer
under gauze, under the custody
of an un-vow; let

the people gawp and jabber.
Chew things over sacramentally.
Under this fine white silk:

nudity.
Under the skin, her vital organs
hymning away.

And the heart's rough justice,
she as He required
pleading guilty,

torn temple
instantly absolved and back on trial.

Margery's Second Wedding

Married –

in a flurry of God

White – brighter than any dress
    decreed to my soul

Such light as could cause loss
    of self-perception, of what comes across

Humanity

I called for Christ, his cross,
but only – barely – caught his voice –

She is my precious love and she feels fear

I had the madness then
to make demand
Where is God's hand

(the furls of it, the rip tides, and the shock
like lightening striking at the heart)

He holds you in it. So it was
that what seemed alien was really us:
His heart so large it was a pulsing cosmos,

the milky way a shimmer in his hand,

and I a flake of nacre
on a whorl of his finger

a solar flare
encircling all that vows.

Wondrous Hot and Delectable

God's a hot flush –
a raw body-rush
of volatile maturity

Flammable nights
in his arms
and the chill of withdrawal

This thermostat
is taken by the grace of his surprise:
upsurge, low-light, pucker –

How measure mirth and awe?
– by the blushful.

Now I, wise to life's cycles
dance, rave, in the guttering pyre
of the power of my name.

'I seem to have always a craving to touch the great human mystery of Time'

(Hope Emily Allen, editor)

It heaves; a great wheel
spewing water, ephemeral gems
heart-refracting, no
human mystery –
we suffer in its spume.

Her ailing priest says: *Damsel,*
Ihesu is ded long sithyn –
one thousand and four hundred years ago
among the stripped trees
he hung. Now not an atom
suffered or sustained.

Heart-refracting
Great water wheel

The priest fades as he speaks.
Out of charity, she keeps
his dessicated words as fallen leaves.

Then the water whips her – *Sir*
hys deth is the body cleaving to its god
as fresch to me as he had
lift me into the palm of life, the sorrow
deyd þis same day
as he told me that he loved
& we awt euyr the work that he did
he gave to her
to han mende of hys kendnes & euvyr thynkyn of

She sees him and more than sees.
She wrote not a word and we read her.
The water softens, quenches, drowns,
þe dolful deth þat he deyd for vs
streams on. The wheel itself
hys kendnes & euvyr refracts,
she says, *eternity.*

'Wher is my name?'

My name is *Creature* to his scribe
I name not him, nor any child
of mine. Only my husband John,
and he who knew my name is gone.

The layering of words in time
makes up a palimpsest so fine
its white gauze moulds me and
its textured silence holds me in.

My book jumps up to hoops of gold
of hagiography. It's grains in folds
as if the worn down glass of years
is sandstuff in the palms and ears.

Life shines in fits and scratches you.
Your words are trapped in amber too.
Things just for then are just for now –
These words are mine and in your power.

'a very dowtyr to me & a modyr also, a syster, a wife, and a spowse'

These are the worlds
unfurled for me; he
Covering with his rich robe
Hovering with his rent robe
    And holding out
His hands, the wounded palms
               indented
With an invisible force
(Those pegs we hang our self-love over,
Frozen nubs of nothing.)

One day I dropped my guard,
And then my husband, sons,
My chickens, little ones.
I gave up my role, furs, gowns,
The names of towns, the company,
the small beer and the night.
I swore to white.

It was then that the world's negative
Showed its silver backing;
from the prayer-and-corner,
The beating heart, the opened
               shrine of the ribs,
the core: I was all
the women I could be to him,
and for each there was a world,
and for each there was a word,
and I was new.

as þow hir hert xulde a brostyn a-sundyr

the thunder of loving the thunder of loving the crack of the whip in the heart without asking the words in my mouth not my own like the set prayers paving the way to the thunder above him the shred of my evidence ripped up and fluttering over the hill are you coming an underling cradled as royalty cherished as progeny all hauled into the hall of discovery watered and streaming like language yet weeping the heart's hot gallop its judders of insight and holding these things up high like Mary pray for us fruit of the narrative hay in the manger a mantra in loops of eternity haloing veins as proof of forever and I am a pulse like a light in the blue white faceted, fabulous fable.

Now I am old I do not cry so much

Now I am old I do not cry so much.
The tempest has relaxed into a lake,
and though I cannot see you I can touch
your spirit, though you feel your body ache.

My transformation is of fire to song
then song to words, then telling all to scribes
who do their craft with ink swept dark and long
across the thirsty parchment which imbibes

The love that pulled my life into its shape.
Oh, I have always been outside the box,
the church, the safe house, and the pilgrim's boat;
I am the wild-lived woman, feral fox,
the gabbling goose whose beak is at your throat.
I pray you: tell the years all I was made.

Into the Voice of a Little Bird which is called a Red-Breast

Flows a thread of silver called a river –
circuits the flimsy frame, lifts the bird
its breast a feathered blush on jealous grass; peaks
through a tiny beak, and forms a song;

something you know like your hands, but have never yet heard;
music at the rite of dawn and dusk you've never known;
a palimpsest flashing its scars; a mirror the sun
an angel unfurling a scroll which is suddenly gone.

Margery's Harbour: A Dramatic Monologue and Songs For Performance with Music by Ken Crandell

Margery's Harbour

...Then the vision left me and I wept like a girl.

Not that I've no experience of life, Good Mother –
I've known – fourteen times! – through my own body's rupture
what it's like to be in on Creation: Impossible
without a Scream fit to raise
the neighbourhood. And if my gossip or the doctor's
there, why, then I'm likely to rip them too –
both verbally and with my hands
pulling away their garments
(endless, maid Bettina's was, a cloth
wound round her like a magic bodkin
suffering all my cries. I vouch for her).
Still, a Brewer's Dozen is enough for any woman.
What with the business, and my husband John,
no wonder I'd be dead on my feet sometimes,
The only comfort to me was my velvets,
swathing me; soaking up those Fears.
Imagine then – there was another rupture.
and this one cast my body into space
where I gasped for very love of life,
and was caressed, amidst my birthing howls,
by a Gorgeous Voice. *My Margery*, He said,
you are my dearest daughter and my wife.
Now what He meant thereby He only knows.

But since He takes two things and makes them one,
so have I, through my body and my tongue,
turned lily-pure again. The white
linen of his love is sewn around me,
and in it I sail.
Strange to say, Good Mother,
that though I've travelled to the pilgrim sites
of a hundred saints, I feel as though
the greatest Ocean Wave is in my own
being. Welling though my ducts and pores,
as salty an absolution as the sea, yet
warmer thereby. As if my very blood's
coagulated into constant weeping. (Am I not
a woman drawing water by the wayside,
to whom He speaks?) And odd to tell, Dear Mother,
that though I travelled on a donkey's back,
driven to crying mercy! – for the blessed
beast was trotting nowhere fast – it still does seem to me
I am the stubbornest thing upon the road:
Lord, yes, I bray and bit, and swiftly kick
those whom the vision bid me to chastise –
those Indolencies who do preen themselves
against His Holy Judgements and Advice,
Good Mother, you are patient with your guest,
I am not used to patience.

My life has fashioned me to seize
what size, what space there is. The words
burst from me, leaving me open
like a raggedy split silk; threads all wrenched
awry. Until my heart is a rip-
tide of pleasure and remorse. And yet –
he promises we shall be knit together
into a finer tapestry. Good Mother,
can you stitch my thoughts into a worthier form?
Your face is shining after all your years
spent in secluded worship.
You have learned to weave
live prayer into your lines.
And now you speak of patience and I see
Mary at her reading, shaping her mouth
into slow O's. You speak of patience
and I hear the simplicity of bells.

You speak of the work of the Holy Ghost
and I see ships: glorious retinues
in great serenity of billowed cloth, all voyaging
towards their each and every special berth.

*And I am steered by kindness and by starlight
into my elected anchorage.*

How Can I Begin

How can I begin to tell
What the voices sang to me
Words that rang the time like bells
Silver rain from golden trees,

What the voices sang. To me
each whisper was an answered prayer.
Silver rain from golden trees
And heaven was a forest there.

Each whisper was an answer. Prayer
had never felt like this before
and heaven was a forest. There
was grace resolving every flaw.

I'd never felt this light before
the rapture ripped my mind apart
was grace resolving every flaw?
I held my breath. He blessed my heart.

The rapture ripped my mind apart
with words that rang the time like bells
I held my breath. He blessed my heart
and now I can begin to tell.

That a Woman Might Speak One Hour on the Love of God

(song lyric version)

He, lyftyng vp hys handys & blyssyng hym, seyd, 'Benedicite. What cowd a woman ocupyn an owyr er tweyn owyrs in the lofe of owyr Lord?'

Five minutes with your palms up-cupped
With woman's words you might have supped

A minute at the burnished table
Here starts *Margery's main fable*!

Twenty minutes at my story:
Priests and bishops in their glory

Enter woodland and get lost
For ten long minutes. Nightfall frost.

Four minutes' midnight warning.
A *Pater Noster*'s worth of mourning.

Six-sixty seconds of delighting
With more laughter than affrighting –

Then a moment's hesitation –
(Three *Hail Marys* and a *Station*)

And my monologue to finish,
Decade's worth of beaded minutes.

Thus as woman will I speak.
… Now *press repeat.*

Song of the Senses

'By this Sweet Smell, Thou Mayest Well Know'
Honey, hops and dew –
The soul's sweet brew.

A petal partly crushed,
That dream, too rushed,

Synaesthesia. Song.
I knew him all along.

Ink, sweat and tears,
The twisted rope of years
Wrung into words,
My scribes – bright birds

Candlewax and water
Sanctity's daughters.

Salt and bitter and wood,
A woman making good,

Telling tales, taking time,
She's the sea's strong wine

Poured for you. Heart, crossed
And nothing is lost.

Margery's Tears

The tears I am afflicted with
like fragments from a crystal ball
through them I see your future life
in them I see your future fall

The teardrops that adorn my face
are pearls of wisdom all from him
who waits at every stopping place
and offers respite from within

A crying woman: who would think
that she could be washed clean from sin
after a long life drowning. Drink
the grace of oceans, learn to swim.
This creature weeps for what is lost,
for those who never reached the land,
for what is broken at such cost
for all who still refuse God's hand.

These tears are praying beads, they shine
with hope of heaven after rain.
Each day a teardrop and a sign
my weeping has not been in vain.

Margery's Travels

Margery travelling
stories unravelling
history, mystery
holy and maddening

Sometimes they say to me
Why do you pray for me
Sometimes they spy on me
Making me cry –

Christian pilgrimage
Wandering hill and ridge
hostels intemperate!
vicars immoderate!

Margery's wearing white
robes that are full and bright
looking for wonders in lands where He walked
singing the book of songs as she was taught
Margery travelling
stories unravelling
history, mystery
holy and maddening

Mystical Margery
never was loved the less
walking and talking she wanted to run,
Nobody seemed to know
where such a soul might go
she was a journey that never was done.

Margery travelling
stories unravelling
history, mystery,
holy and maddening.

'When I Speak These Words'

(text for multi-voice performance from a Creative Practice Day for the Facility, London Metropolitan University, January 2011)

When I speak these words
They cross the border of my mouth

Having travelled through the throat's tunnel
A few books packed on their backs

But no passport intact
Each word slips   invisible
Into air

Having cuffed a few ears
With whispered subversions

Words: burnt stars
From old skies –

Each has travelled
Light-millions of years
To drop
Vulnerable
into our vulnerable
Hands
Like white-hot gems
Which seek a constellation.
What you see is difficult to say:
I behold a figure cross-legged on a ledge
Head bent
Hands clasped in meditation
You can see nothing
But a madwoman's cap.

Margery walks down the aisle like a breath seeking meaning
She's one-line phrase
Married to a space break

You're not supposed

                   I couldn't say

You're really here

                   I couldn't stay

I want to cry

                   You're not allowed

I'm on a pilgrimage

                   You are too proud

A story with its back to the wall will tell you anything

Hold your tongue. Take to the elements. Promise
you'll get there in time.